KS2

Honest

A Cherrytree Book

Designed and produced by A S Publishing

First published 1996
by Cherrytree Press Ltd
Windsor Bridge Road
Bath BA2 3AX

Copyright © Cherrytree Press Ltd 1996

British Library Cataloguing in Publication Data
Amos, Janine
    Honest - (Viewpoints)
    1. Honesty - Juvenile literature 2. Moral development
    Juvenile literature
    I. Title
    155.4'1825

ISBN 07451 5284 8

Printed and bound in Italy by LEGO Spa, Vicenza

All rights reserved. No part of this publication may be reproduced, stored in a retrieval system or transmitted, in any form or by any means without the prior permission in writing of the publisher, nor be otherwise circulated in any form of binding or cover other than that in which it is published and without a similar condition including this condition being imposed on the subsequent purchaser.

Honest

Two stories seen from
two points of view

by Janine Amos
Illustrated by Gwen Green

CHERRYTREE BOOKS

Tom and the new bike

"Time to go!" thought Tom, looking at the big kitchen clock. Tom had promised to call for his friend Jamie. There was no school today, and they were taking their bikes to the park.

Jamie came to the door with a big smile. "Look at this!" he said, proudly. "It's my birthday present from my dad!"

Tom stared. Jamie wheeled out a brand new mountain bike. It was the smartest bike Tom had ever seen.

"Wow!" gasped Tom. "Can I have a go after you?"

"OK," said Jamie, pulling on his coat.

"Hold it!" called Jamie's mum, coming into the hallway. "Don't forget your doctor's appointment is at ten o' clock. I'll pick you up from the park."

"All right," nodded Jamie, guiding his new bike carefully through the door.

At the park, Tom watched Jamie ride round and round for ages. The new bike looked really smooth. Tom couldn't wait to try it out for himself.

When Jamie's mum arrived in the car, Jamie came sailing over to Tom.

"I've got to go," he said, getting off. "Watch this for me until I get back." He stood the bike against the railings and got out his padlock.

"Don't lock it up!" said Tom. "Let me ride it while you're at the doctor's."

Jamie thought about it.

"Promise you'll look after it!" he said.

Tom nodded.

Tom was soon whizzing round and round on the new bike. Some big boys wandered over to watch him. Tom went faster and faster. He felt brave and strong. Up into the air he went, the whole bike left the ground. Tom knew he was showing off, but he didn't care.

Crash! When Tom hit the iron gate he came right off. He lay on the ground and rubbed his leg. He watched the older boys walk away, sniggering.

Then Tom remembered Jamie's bike. It lay beside him, with the wheels slowly spinning round. There was a deep dent in the shiny frame. Tom groaned.

Tom examined the bike in horror.

"It's spoilt!" he whispered, rubbing his hand along the dented frame. Carefully, he lifted the bike up. He propped it against the railings, and gently wiped off the dust.

After a while, Tom got back on his own bike. Slowly he circled round, waiting for Jamie.

It wasn't long before Jamie came running towards him. Tom could feel his heart banging in his chest. Straight away, Jamie went over to the bike.

"What's happened to it?" he shouted.

Tom didn't say anything. He felt a bit sick.

Jamie came up very close. His eyes were full of tears.

"How did it get dented?" he screamed. He pulled at Tom's sleeve.

"I don't know!" said Tom quickly. "It was some big boys. They did it. And now they've run off."

Tom looked down. He didn't want Jamie to see his face.

"Liar!" shouted Jamie. "You did it, and you're too scared to tell me!"

Jamie was sniffing now. Tom hoped he wasn't going to cry.
"I'm going home," said Jamie at last.

Tom watched his friend cycle off through the gate. He felt cold and shaky. He'd made everything much worse.

Turn to page 18 to read Jamie's side of things.

Annie and the project

It was the start of the new school term. Mrs Turner was giving the class a writing project.

"It's to be all about your holiday," she told them.

"I went to Disney World!" shouted Daniel. Annie sighed. Daniel always went somewhere exciting.

Mrs Turner carried on. "It doesn't matter if you didn't go anywhere! Everyone had a holiday from school. Tell me about yours. You can add drawings, photographs - anything you like."

On the way home, Annie talked about it with her friend Meg.

"It's easy to write about a holiday at Disney World!" moaned Annie. "I only went to the beach with my cousin."

"That's OK," replied Meg. "Mine will be about the seaside too. I think I'll put some shells in. I collected lots."

Later, Annie took out her project file. "I went to the seaside with Laura," she wrote. Then she got stuck and made a face.

"Perhaps Meg would like to come over this weekend?" suggested Annie's mum. "You could work on your projects together."

"Brill!" said Annie.

At the weekend, Annie took out her project book again. She sucked her pencil and frowned. She stared out of the window. Then she closed her file and turned on the television. Soon she had forgotten all about her project.

Meg arrived after lunch. She was carrying a thick folder and an enormous plastic bag.

"What's in there?" asked Annie.

"My project!" said Meg proudly.

Annie chewed her lip. "I haven't even started yet," she worried.

Annie watched Meg begin to write, just like that!

"It's not fair!" thought Annie. "I can't think of anything to put and Meg's done loads already."

Then Annie's mum came in with juice and biscuits. She stopped to look at Meg's folder.

"It's great!" she said. "You have worked hard, Meg."

Annie nibbled at a biscuit and pretended not to listen. At that moment she didn't like Meg very much.

"Could I wash my seashells in your sink?" Meg was asking.

"Of course," replied Annie's mum. "Come along with me."

Annie sat at the table on her own. Slowly, she got up and went across to Meg's folder. Carefully, she opened it and looked inside. Her mum was right. It was brilliant! Meg had written a diary all about her holiday. There were drawings, a poem about seaweed, and a picture map of the beach.

Annie could hear her mum and Meg talking in the kitchen. She grabbed a pencil and some paper. Quickly she copied as much of Meg's project as she could.

After a while, Meg came back with the clean shells. Annie was sitting in her own place busy writing. She kept her arm round her work so that Meg couldn't see.

Annie was quiet all through tea. Whenever Meg looked at her, Annie looked away. She felt bad about herself. She couldn't wait for Meg to go home.

On Monday morning, Annie's class took their projects into school. Annie put her folder down on the desk. She wanted to give it in quickly, before anyone asked to look.

Just then, Meg came running over. "Let's see yours!" she said, pulling Annie's file towards her.

Meg flicked through the pages, while Annie stood and stared.

"You cheat!" screamed Meg at last and flung the project back.

Annie's face burned. She wanted to run away. She wished she'd never seen Meg's project.

For Meg's point of view go to page 24.

Jamie and the new bike

Jamie sat in the kitchen, waiting for his friend Tom to arrive. From where he was sitting, Jamie could just see his new bike standing in the hallway.

"It's brilliant, isn't it, Mum?" said Jamie for the tenth time.

Jamie's mum smiled. "You can take it for a quick ride. Then we'll have to go to the doctor's. You need something for that cough," she told him.

The doorbell rang and Jamie dashed to answer it. "Just wait till you see this, Tom!" he called.

Later, Jamie and his mum sat in the waiting room at the doctor's. It was hot and stuffy. Jamie didn't trust the air in the room. It was bound to make his cough worse!

Jamie thought again about his bike. It was a special birthday present from his dad. Jamie's dad lived miles away, and Jamie didn't see him very often. Sometimes the presents his dad gave him were a bit babyish. This time, though, he'd got it just right.

Jamie thought of Tom riding on the new bike. Jamie didn't really mind lending it. Tom was his friend. But it still felt a bit funny. Jamie kicked his heels against the seat.

"Hurry up, Doctor!" he said.

After the doctor's Jamie's mum drove him back to the park. As soon as he could, Jamie leapt out.

He could see Tom riding round and round in the distance. His own bike was leaning against the railings. Jamie ran towards it.

Jamie saw at once that his bike was dented. He stood and stared.

Jamie felt dizzy. There was a strange fluttering deep in his stomach. His face burned. He was shaking with anger.

Jamie ran over to Tom, shouting. He wanted to pull Tom off his bike. He wanted to hit Tom hard. Instead, he screamed at him, "What happened?"

Jamie waited for Tom to explain. He waited for Tom to say he was sorry. But Tom looked away.

Then Tom started muttering. He was making excuses. Jamie could tell that he was lying. Jamie felt both sad and angry at once. He thought he'd burst, but there was nothing he could do.

Suddenly the tears came. Quickly, Jamie pulled himself on to his bike and set off home.

Meg and the project

As soon as Meg got home, she hunted for her seashells. There they were, still in the plastic bucket she'd taken on holiday.

Meg's little brother Sam wanted them. "No!" said Meg. "These are important. They're for my project."

After tea, Meg looked at the photographs they'd taken at the seaside. Soon she was remembering the campsite at the beach, and the sand and the sunshine. She started to write.

She wrote about the picnic they'd had at the ruined castle. She remembered how they'd been attacked by wasps. And how exciting it had been to sleep in a tent.

After a while, Meg's dad came to see how she was getting on. He read a few pages. "You've written it like a diary," he said, smiling. "That's a clever idea. Why don't you draw a map, like the one I lost."

Meg was pleased with his suggestion. She drew a map with a little green triangle to show their tent, and lots of blue squiggles for the sea.

Later, Meg went to get a glass of milk. When she came back, Sam was in her room. He was looking at her map, and drawing on it with a thick felt pen!

Meg shouted.

"Poor Meg!" said her mum, rushing in. "Sam didn't mean to. He thought he was helping."

When Sam had gone to bed, Meg drew the map all over again. Then she put the folder safely away, out of Sam's reach.

On Saturday afternoon, Meg went over to Annie's house. She liked it there. Annie's brother was ten. He didn't scribble on your drawings or talk all the time, like Sam.

Meg laid her project down on the table. She saw Annie watching her. She knew Annie was looking at her thick folder - and wondering what was inside.

On Monday, Meg took her project to school in her backpack. She could feel it bumping against her shoulders as she walked. She couldn't wait to show it to Mrs Turner.

At school, Meg saw Annie come into the classroom. She was holding a big folder against her chest. Meg waved. But Annie didn't come over. Instead, she put her folder down on the desk and kept her hand on it. Suddenly Meg badly wanted to open it up and read it.

Meg ran across and opened Annie's file. She turned the pages, one by one. It was a seaside holiday diary, just like her own. There was a poem about seaweed, a picture map, and some seashells in a plastic bag. All Meg's best ideas were there - in Annie's handwriting.

Meg could feel a buzzing in her ears. She slammed the folder back on the desk. Her whole body was shaking. She blinked back tears. Annie had spoilt everything.

Jamie says

"Tom crashed my bike. But he pretended he didn't do it. He wasn't honest with me. That really hurt. He's supposed to be my friend."

Tom says

"I was scared to tell Jamie what I'd done. But lying only made it worse. I'll tell him it was an accident. I'll say I'm sorry. Maybe then he'll like me again."

Meg says

"I wanted everyone to know that the diary idea was mine. But Annie was sneaky. She stole all my ideas. Now my project doesn't look so special."

Annie says

"It felt wrong to copy. But I couldn't think what to write. And Meg's ideas were so good. I didn't know she'd be so upset, though. I'm sorry now. I'll never cheat again."

Being Honest

Tom was sorry for denting Jamie's bike. But he was scared of what his friend would say. Tom tried to blame someone else instead.

Annie was dishonest, too. She didn't spend time on her own project. She copied her friend's.

Honesty isn't about looking for the easy way out. It might seem like a good idea at the time to lie or cheat to solve a problem. But in the long term, you feel guilty and bad about yourself.

Honesty takes courage and hard work. It isn't easy to own up when someone's cross, or to struggle with a piece of work you're finding tough. But honest people feel good about themselves, and other people know they can trust them. Honesty is an important part of friendship.